JOSEPH ANDREW MAR(

EFFORTL]
ENLIGHTENMENT

HOW TO INSTANTANEOUSLY AWAKEN TO THE SIMPLE CLARITY RIGHT WHERE YOU ARE

A LETTER
FROM
DOUGLAS HARDING

JOSEPH ANDREW MARCELLO

EFFORTLESS, ENLIGHTENMENT
HOW TO INSTANEOUSLY AWAKEN TO
THE SIMPLE CLARITY RIGHT WHERE YOU ARE

ISBN 9781725835900

Printed in the United States of America

JOSEPH ANDREW MARCELLO

My admonition is this: be a Great Fool!
A petty little fool is nothing but a worldling.
But a Great Fool is a Buddha!

Sogaku Harada

*

To the 'Great Fool' that was Douglas Edison Harding, who so ardently, even beseechingly, strove to have us join him in his foolishness.

And to those, touched and inspired by his vision, who, alas, never had the opportunity to experience the power of his personal presence and encouragement, this book is dedicated.

"Those who, either now or after I am dead, shall be lamps unto themselves, relying upon themselves only and not relying upon any external help, but holding fast to the truth as their lamp, and seeking their salvation in the truth alone, and shall not look for assistance to any one besides themselves, it is they, Ananda, among my bhikkhus, who shall reach the very topmost height! But they must be passionate to learn."

Attributed to the Buddha, on his deathbed

JOSEPH ANDREW MARCELLO

PREFACE

As Douglas Harding might very well himself have said, the title of this book is no mere come-on, no hook or 'clickbait' put forth merely for the sake of capturing the attention of potential readers. Rather, it is the ardent, bracing conviction of a man who truly knows whereof he speaks: that a totally, radically new view of oneself and the universe awaits—indeed, is all but imminent—if only we would allow ourselves to look

The reason for the sharing of the letter was written to the author almost 45 years ago is that, in spite of its personal nature, it is, by virtue of its power and clarity, a gift that rightly belongs to all.

Douglas' words and insights are hardly any one person's proprietary possession, least of all my own. In the end, they are for the world, and it is for the world they are now made available–with, it should be noted, the imprimatur, subsequently, of Douglas' personally-tendered blessings, free of any legal or literary constraints, beyond the proviso that, should I ever wish to share his words, either privately or in published form, they be presented in their original content and context, as written, This request has been honored through the inclusion of a facsimile of Douglas' original document.

Indeed, the beauty of his message is that its self-evidentiality leaves virtually no way to miss—much

1

less misrepresent—it; one has only to point it out, step aside and—with apologies to Lennon & McCartney—let it be.   For his graciousness, generosity and encouragement, Douglas continues to have my deep and lasting gratitude.

Some readers may wish to to note that a far fuller edition of the back story behind the writing of this letter—and its dramatic impact upon the writer, replete with many personal anecdotes and reflections—may be found in the prior volume in this series, *You See the Totally Obvious & Simple Clarity Right Where You are When You WANT To—A Letter From Douglas Harding; A Personal Memoir.*

Joseph Marcello

JOSEPH ANDREW MARCELLO

We only see what we want to see; we only hear what we want to hear. Our belief system is just like a mirror that only shows us what we believe.

Don Miguel Ruiz

I have as much authority as the Pope. I just don't have as many people who believe it.

George Carlin

'But I never looked like that!'
 - How do you know? What is the 'you' you might or might not look like? Where do you find it—by which morphological or expressive calibration? Where is your authentic body? You are the only one who can never see yourself except as an image; you never see your eyes unless they are dulled by the gaze they rest upon in the mirror or the lens (I am interested in seeing my eyes only when they look at you): even and especially for your own body, you are condemned to the repertoire of its images.

— *Roland Barthes*

"I see," said the blind man—but he couldn't see at all!

Anonymous

EFFORTLESS, ENLIGHTENMENT
HOW TO INSTANEOUSLY AWAKEN TO
THE SIMPLE CLARITY RIGHT WHERE YOU ARE

DOROTHY
Oh, will you help me? Can you help me?

GLINDA, GOOD WITCH OF THE SOUTH
You don't need to be helped any longer.
You've always had the power to go back to Kansas.

DOROTHY
I have?

SCARECROW
Then why didn't you tell her before?

GLINDA
Because she wouldn't have believed me. She had to
learn it for herself.

TIN MAN
What have you learned, Dorothy?

DOROTHY
Well, I -- I think that it -- that. . . if I ever go looking
for my heart's desire again, I won't look any further
than my own backyard. Because if it isn't there, I
never really lost it to begin with! Is that right?

GLINDA
That's all it is!

F.L. Baum, author & Noel Langley, screen writer The
Wizard of Oz

XXII

Traveler, there is no path.
The path is made by walking.

Traveler, the path is your footprints,
And nothing more.
Traveler, there is no path
The path is made by walking.
By walking you make a path
And turning, you look back
At a way you will never again tread,
Traveler, there is no road
Only trailing wakes in the sea.

Antonio Machado

*

Not knowing the way,
I'm going the way
With open hands,
With open hands

EFFORTLESS, ENLIGHTENMENT
HOW TO INSTANEOUSLY AWAKEN TO
THE SIMPLE CLARITY RIGHT WHERE YOU ARE

I

ORIGINAL LETTER

SHOLLOND HILL

NACTON

NEAR IPSWICH, SUFFOLK

NACTON 301

Oct 31 '72

Dear Joseph,

Your fascinating letter gratefully received. I'll do my best to answer some of it now, but, hopefully we can meet before too long. That will be much better than written words, or any words.

I have a 'headless' friend who is a friend of Vimala's. She is surely a fine person, & I hope to meet her.

I think the "problem" with these wonderful people – like Ramana, [Krishnamurti, Vimala]— is that their admirers/devotees/friends feel they haven't 'got there', or even could never 'get there', the way the 'Master' has. And this in spite of the fact that the 'Master' keeps saying "what are you waiting for?" "If you can't see who you are, who can?" "It's easier to see the Self than anything out there!" "If it's attained it will be lost: Enlightenment is seeing what you already are & have always been." R.M. talked this all the time in his

7

2

later years — + the more he did so the more
his disciples fixed their love + attention on him,
instead of the One who was attending to him!

If I may say so, I feel pretty sure you see
the totally obvious + simple Clarity right where
you are, when you _want_ to! (If you doubt this,
please try 5 simple tests:-
① Get into one end of a translucent paper bag,
c. 12" long x 24" dia, with a friend at the other
end, and see what's
(not) at _your_ end.
Isn't it wide open?

② Put on glasses slowly + see what happens
to the 2 'eyeholes'. How many eyes are you
looking out of, in your own 1st hand experience, now?
③ Locate your face — in the mirror.
④ Looking down (up) your shirtfront, see where it
fades out.
⑤ Slowly put on card with head-shaped,
head-sized hole in it. The small
void for seeing becomes the infinite   12"
Void for seeing with.)   12"

When you are seeing into your Absence thus,
you _can't_ do it wrong, or see it less clearly
than I do or the Buddha did! There are no

8

3

degrees of vividness or Enlightenment. No progress. Where progress does come in is :—

① The continuity of your seeing. At first it is sure to be intermittent. You have to go on doing it till it becomes quite natural & steady.

② The effect on your mind / body / environment. Obviously, this is gradual & cumulative. We are so impatient! We want to feel good, now!

All ways to 'enlightenment' have their pros & cons. The pros of this way are

① Precision, Indubitability. You can't doubt what ~~you see right where~~ you are, or the genuineness of your seeing — while it lasts.

② Confidence. You rely on no one outside.

③ Transmissability. You can show people (using paper bag above, or any other way) beyond doubt how it is where they are. No degrees of seeing, or imperfect transmission.

④ Accessibility. You have no excuse for not looking at the Spot you occupy.

⑤ Fun. The truth is hilarious!

Do you have the Harper & Row edition of the No Head book (95c.), which contains a useful Postscript? (published March '72) Incidentally, though the Hierarchy was essential for me, + contains much of value; for most people it is surely full of red herrings. Don't get side-tracked.

Much of your letter is, very understandably, concerned with psychological matters. May I comment, using a Gnostic myth :-

King's son comes down to Egypt to find the Pearl of Self-realisation. Forgets his Father + thinks he's an Egyptian. Is reminded of his task. Locates pearl at bottom of lake, guarded by a Serpent. __By-passes__ Serpent, seizes Pearl + returns to Father.....
He could have (a) fought serpent (ascetic discipline) or (b) chatted up the serpent (psychological investigation / therapy / watching the mind, etc). Instead, he went straight for the Pearl, when the Serpent wasn't looking. Now, armed with the Pearl, he has in it a real Serpent - taming charm. The serpent doesn't become a pussy cate overnight, but does know his Master.

5

(Cf. Ramana: the answer to every problem isn't at its level — it's seeing who has the problem.) (a) fighting the serpent & (b) engaging in a dialogue with him, are just what he loves, & go on interminably. Nothing much happens. That's what he loves!

You ask: surely the hero must be cool & brave enough to dive past that dragon? Well, I've know people who have been terribly disturbed / anxious / problem-ridden / ~~minded, yet able & willing, not only~~ to grasp the Pearl, but to value it, & ~~then~~ use it on the dragon. His response is often disappointing & slow, but it is real. This isn't papering over one's problems, or suppressing them. Armed with the Pearl, they are illuminated by it — out there; here one is the Pearl, & free!

———— # ————

It is essential that we meet. I go to the U.S. generally in the spring, but nothing is fixed for '73 yet. Are you likely to come here, before then? If so, You will be very welcome indeed here. We have no name, organisation, guru, but we do have a place here where friends come & meet together. The usual thing is that, weekends, there are up to 20 or so folks here. They bring some food & if possible sleeping bags. It's all free — which is terrible psychology — they tell me!

The reasons we meet are, mainly, to reinforce each other's 'seeing' (it can be contagious) & gain confidence in who we really are. One of the less important reasons why You should join us if you can is that You would observe how totally 'democratic' this way is. You would see that Douglas (warts & all) is nothing special at all, & You would no longer be tempted to look at him, instead of what he's pointing to — namely, the one who's now reading this sentence. No room to thank You for so much in Your letter, such and quotes. — — — Douglas H.

JOSEPH ANDREW MARCELLO

II

LETTER (TEXT VERSION)

Dear Joseph,

Your fascinating letter gratefully received. I'll do my best to answer some of it now, but hopefully we can meet before too long. That will be much better than written words – or any words.

I have a 'headless' friend who is a friend of Vimala's. She is surely a fine person, & I hope to meet her.

I think the "problem" with these wonderful people—like Ramana (Krishnamurti/Vimala}—is that their admirers/ devotees/friends feel they haven't 'got there', or even could never 'get there', the way the 'Master' has – And this is spite of the fact that the 'Master' keeps saying 'What are you waiting for?' "If you can't see who you are, who can?" "It's easier to see the Self than anything out there!" "If it's attained it will be lost"; Enlightenment" is seeing what you already are & have always been." R.M. talked all the time in his later years – & the more he did so the more his disciples fixed their love & attention on <u>him</u> instead of the One who was attending to him!

14

If I may say so, I feel pretty sure you see the totally obvious & simple Clarity right where you are, when you want to! (If you doubt this, please try 5 simple tests: –

(1) Get into one end of a translucent paper bag, c. 12" long x 24" dia., with a friend at the other end, and see what's (not) at your end.
Isn't it wide open?

(2) Put on glasses slowly and see what happens to its 2 'eyeholes'. How many eyes are you looking out of in your own firsthand experience, now?

(3) Locate your face – in the mirror.

(4) Looking down (up) your shirtfront, see where it fades out.

(5) Slowly put on card with head-shaped, head-sized hole in it. The small void for seeing becomes the infinite Void for seeing with. When you are seeing into your Absence thus, you can't do it wrong, or see it less clearly than I do or the Buddha did.

There are no degrees of voidness or Enlightenment. No progress – where progress does come in is: –

(1) the continuity of your seeing. At first it is sure to be intermittent. You have to go on doing it 'till (sp) it

becomes quite natural & steady.

(1) the effect on your mind/body/environment. Obviously, this is gradual & cumulative. We are so impatient! We want to feel good, now!

All ways to 'Enlightenment' have their pros & cons. The pros of this way are

(1) Precision, indubitability. You can't doubt what you see right where you are, or the genuineness of the seeing – while it lasts.

(2) Confidence. You rely on no one outside.

(3) Transmissability (sp). You can show people (using paper bag above, or any other way) beyond doubt how it is where they are. No degrees of seeing, or imperfect transmission.

(4) Accessibility. You have no excuse for not looking at the Spot you occupy.

(5) Fun. The truth is hilarious!

Do you have the Harper & Row edition of the No Head book (95 c.) which contains a useful Postscript?

(published March '72) Incidentally, though the Hierarchy was essential for me, & contains much of value, for most people it is surely full of red herrings. Don't get side-tracked.

Much of your letter is, very understandably, concerned with psychological matters. May I comment, using a Gnostic myth: –

King's son comes down to Egypt to find the Pearl of Self-realisation (sp) Forgets his Father & thinks he's an Egyptian. Is reminded of his task. Locates pearl at bottom of lake guarded by a Serpent. <u>Bypasses</u> Serpent, seizes Pearl & returns to Father. . . .

He could have (a) fought serpent (ascetic discipline) or (b) chatted up the serpent (psycholical {sp: 'psychological)} investigation /therapy /watching the mind, etc). Instead, he went straight for the Pearl, when the Serpent wasn't looking. Now, armed with the Pearl, he has in it a real Serpent-taming charm. The serpent doesn't become a pussycat overnight, but does know his Master.

(Cf. Ramana: The answer to your problem isn't at its level – it's seeing who has the problem.)

(a) Fighting the serpent & (b) engaging in a 'dialogue' with him, are just what he loves, & go on interminably. Nothing much happens. That's what he loves!

You ask: surely the hero must be cool & be brave enough to dive past that dragon? Well, I've known people who have been <u>terribly</u> disturbed/anxious/problem-ridden/suicidal, yet able & willing not only to grasp the Pearl, but to value it, & use it on the dragon His response is often disappoint & slow, but it is real. This isn't papering over one's problems, or suppressing them. Armed with the Pearl, they are illuminated by it – out there; here one <u>is</u> the Pearl, & free!

It is essential that we meet. I go the U.S. generally in the spring, but nothing is fixed for '73 yet. Are you likely to come here before then? If so, you will be very welcome indeed here. We have no name, organization, guru, but we do have a place here where friends come & meet together. The usual thing is that, weekends, there are up to 20 or so folks here. They bring some food & if possible sleeping bags – it's all free – which is terrible psychology – they tell me!

The reasons we meet are, mainly, to reinforce each others' 'seeing' (it's extremely contagious), gain confidence in who we really are. One of the less important reasons why you should join us if you can is that you would observe how totally 'democratic' this way is. You would see that Douglas (warts & all) is nothing special at all, & would no longer be tempted to look at him, instead of What he's point to – namely, the one who's now reading this sentence.

No room to thank you for so much in your letter, such good quotes - - - - -

Douglas H

EFFORTLESS, ENLIGHTENMENT
HOW TO INSTANEOUSLY AWAKEN TO
THE SIMPLE CLARITY RIGHT WHERE YOU ARE

The Time Before Death

Friend, hope for the Guest while you are alive.
Jump into experience while you are alive!
Think... and think... while you are alive.
What you call "salvation" belongs to the time
      before death.

If you don't break your ropes while you're alive,
do you think ghosts will do it after?

The idea that the soul will join with the ecstatic
just because the body is rotten --
that is all fantasy.
What is found now is found then.
If you find nothing now,
you will simply end up with an apartment in the
     City of Death.
If you make love with the divine now, in the next
life you will have the face of satisfied desire.

So plunge into the truth, find out who the Teacher is,
Believe in the Great Sound!

Kabir says this: When the Guest is being searched for,
it is the intensity of the longing for the Guest
that does all the work.

Look at me, and you will see a slave of that intensity.

JOSEPH ANDREW MARCELLO

Kabir

There is a Reality which is Indivisible.
One, Alone, the Source and Being of all;
Not a thing, nor even a mind,
but pure Spirit or clear Consciousness;
and we are That and nothing but That,
for That is our true Nature.
And the only way to find It is to look steadily within,
eternal life itself.

Douglas Harding

BIBLIOGRAPHY

Writings by Douglas Harding:

The Hierarchy of Heaven and Earth, A New Diagram of Man in the Universe. Faber & Faber, 1952. (Preface by C.S. Lewis.) Abridged paperback edition. Available as an eBook.

The Hierarchy of Heaven and Earth. The Shollond Trust, 1998. Reproduction of original full manuscript, now out of print. The full manuscript is now available as a downloadable pdf. A truly amazing book.

Visible Gods. 1955. Available as an eBook.

The Universe Revalued. The Saturday Evening Post, 1961. (Article.)

On Having No Head, An Introduction to Zen in the West. London Buddhist Society, 1961. Available as a downloadable audio book. Also available as an eBook

Religions of the World. Heinemann, 1966, edition 2. ebook.

The Face Game. Bulletin of the International Transactional Analysis Assoc. April, 1967. (Article.)

The Toolkit for Testing the Incredible Hypothesis. Shollond Publications, 1972. (Out of print.)

The Science of the 1st Person. Shollond Publications, 1974. Available as an eBook. Also available as a paperback from The Shollond Trust.

The Youniverse Explorer model and audio tape. Shollond Publications, 1976. A new version has been produced in 2014 and is now available to purchase.

The Hidden Gospel. 1976. Available as an eBook

On Having No Head. (Video.) Shollond Publications, 1980.

The Little Book of Life and Death. First published by Penguin, Arkana, 1988. Also available as an

Head Off Stress. Penguin, Arkana, 1990. Also available as an eBook.

The Trial of the Man who said he was God. Penguin, Arkana, 1992. Paperback. Available as an eBook

The Spectre in the Lake. Head Exchange Press, 1996. Also available as an eBook;

Look For Yourself. Head Exchange Press, 1996. Paperback. Available as an eBook

Face to No-Face. Inner Directions, 2000. Edited by David Lang.

To Be and Not To Be. Watkins, 2002. Available as a paperback and an eBook

Open to the Source. Inner Directions, 2005. Edited by Richard Lang. Available as a paperback.

The Turning Point. 2006. Available as an eBook.

THE AUTHOR

Joseph Marcello is an award-winning composer who has explored paths to awakening since early adolescence, studying, in addition to Douglas Harding, with such mentors as mystic and psychologist Karlfried Graf von Durckheim. author of *Hara, the Vital Centre of Man*, Krishnamurti's protégé, Vimala Thakar, whose awakening is documented in her *On an Eternal Voyage*, Sachindra Majumdar in New York, author of *Yoga, Principles & Practices*, and Paramhansa Yogananda's disciple, Roy Eugene Davis, author of *This is Reality*.

He has authored and edited some 8 books on well-being, subtle energies and awakening, including *Life More Abundant; the Science of Zhineng Qigong, Living Vision—the Secret Teachings of Neville Goddard, The Healing Power of Pyramids, Elixir of the Ageless* and *The Hindu Secrets of Virility & Rejuvenation.* He lives on a pine clad hill in Western Massachusetts just below the New Hampshire and Vermont borders, and adores the shoulder-to-shoulder presence of the twenty-odd cockatiels and parakeets he has bred and hand-fed through 5 generations of lineage.

He may be contacted at JosephMarcello@verizon.net.

EFFORTLESS, ENLIGHTENMENT
HOW TO INSTANEOUSLY AWAKEN TO
THE SIMPLE CLARITY RIGHT WHERE YOU ARE

Printed in Great Britain
by Amazon